ESCAPE ED

UNLOCKING STUDENT ACHIEVEMENT

KRISTEN KOPPERS, M. ED., NBCT

BRIAN COSTELLO

Copyright © 2022 by Kristen Koppers & Brian Costello
Published by EduMatch®
PO Box 150324, Alexandria, VA 22315
www.edumatchpublishing.com

All rights reserved. No portion of this book may be reproduced in any form without permission from the publisher, except as permitted by U.S. copyright law. For permissions contact sarah@edumatch.org.

These books are available at special discounts when purchased in quantities of 10 or more for use as premiums, promotions fundraising, and educational use. For inquiries and details, contact the publisher: sarah@edumatch.org.

ISBN: 978-1-953852-43-4

CONTENTS

Brief History of Breakout Boxes	vii
Introduction	ix
"We Escaped"	1
Cross-Curricular Work	5
Cognitive Learning by Engaging Students	13
Collaboration Leads to Team Building and Communication	17
Comprehension through Cognitive Learning	23
Creating your Own Games	27
Setting up 'The Game'	63
Templates for Breakout Lessons	67
References	77
About the Authors	79
Also by Kristen Koppers	81
Also by Brian Costello	83

Dedication

Kristen - *I can't explain how much my Professional Learning Network has helped me grow in the last five years. I dedicate this book to not only one person but to my entire PLN because without them, I would not be where I am at now. My passion for education consistently changes. My husband, Kristopher, and my son, Jakob, continue to guide me through all my ups and downs. Lastly, I am glad I can work on different breakout activities with Erin Mueller (@emueller1860) and Maggie Maslowski (@MaggieMaslowski) with their continued support and ideas. I am thankful for my co-author, Brian Costello, who agreed to write this book with me. But I cannot forget the friendship with my publisher, Sarah Thomas, who has always put others first.*

Brian - *Writing this book would never have been conceivable without my amazing friends from the Google Innovator cohort in Toronto 2016, who introduced me to my first experience with Breakouts and Escape Rooms. My love for these activities was created there. Also, to my mentor and friend Sarah Thomas, who has provided me with countless opportunities to succeed and grow. Finally, to my family, Lindsay, Emily, and Lucas. They are the reason I push so hard to be successful in all that I do.*

We would like to thank Breakout EDU for their help in not only creating this epic gamification to increase pedagogy skills but allowing us to create such a book with your help.

BRIEF HISTORY OF BREAKOUT BOXES

Education everywhere and anywhere there is learning. Using Breakout boxes in an "escape type classroom" is the newest phenomenon of creating gamification in schools. James Sanders founded and started Breakout.Edu after he attended "an escape room with a few high school students and teachers in 2015 and witnessed some amazing collaboration and critical thinking as a few of the high school kids were trying (and failing multiple times) to open a lock based on some clues provided" (Breakout EDU, 2019). Breakout Edu was the first to pioneer and introduce the concept with the first game being played in April 2015. Sanders thought about creating a way where learning about "failures" did not take away from student learning.

Breakout EDU transformed from a small group of educators with an idea to a quickly growing company. Between the first game in 2015 and now, the company has grown by leaps and bounds. The community of educators using, supporting, and sharing their creations has exploded as the company has continued to develop. "Breakout EDU is a physical game kit and platform where students work together to solve various puzzles to open a locked box, similar to an escape room. You can use Breakout kits in every subject area and grade level" (Breakout EDU, 2019).

This new phenomenon exploded into the mainstream with an escape room bus at ISTE in 2016. It has taken over schools and classrooms ever since. There have been many attempts to recreate the style and purpose of escape room games in the classroom since. This trend in creating learning opportunities stems from the ideas of James Sanders and Mark Hammons.

After the success of the original Breakout Edu boxes, educators worldwide looked to find more ways to enjoy the engagement and learning with these great games. That desire sparked the generation of Digital Breakouts. Creating breakout games on a digital platform brought new ways to access games, create material, and engage students. Digital Breakout games were transformed into an official platform for Breakout Edu and have been a great way to bring the challenge to the world.

Since the conception of Breakout EDU, teachers across the globe have been creating lessons at every level for every course. Social media sites have even emerged with groups focusing on breakout activities, along with many websites offering different ways to create a lesson, clues, and combinations.

Are you ready to Breakout?

INTRODUCTION

I (Kristen) started to use breakout box-type escape rooms three years ago after attending a conference in Southern Illinois. At the conference, there was a session on breaking out of education. While I knew what escape rooms were, I wanted to see how educators were able to take escape-type rooms into the classroom. My goal was to "breakout" of my own box to try new educational tools that did not overtake the lesson. I ordered five boxes, with all the locks, through a grant for my classroom. Although I wasn't too sure how to create lessons for my class, I was willing to research and learn. I focused on secondary education to make sure they were level appropriate and made sure they were a part of the learning. I have to admit that I actually never played the game before buying them; however, I was determined to learn as my students did.

Because I am focused on students' learning within their own group, I made sure that the clues were different in each box, including the lock combinations. This made my work a little harder as I had to create anywhere from 25 - 40 different clues and 25-40 different lock combinations. While it did take some time to create a lesson, it was well worth it in the end. Teaching high school English, the breakout boxes focused on the end of the unit readings. The first breakout box that I created was with a colleague based on two different dystopian novels. Students were to connect with other sophomores from a different class to solve the clues. This created a cross-collaboration between the two classes of students.

Since the first breakout box, I have created several others in the last two years. In all three of my breakout boxes (or sometimes classroom escape rooms), I included some type of digital component. Students learn to collaborate with each other in order to solve the clues; however, adding in the music with the time counting down makes the game more interesting as students not only try to compete against each other but against the music and clock. This type of gamification in the classroom adds to the authenticity of learning. At first, I was hesitant to use any type of breakout boxes in my classroom during instruction time. However, as more and more teachers began using them, I found the opportunity to create a gamified activity where students could collaborate with each other and learn from their own mistakes while I was monitoring their progress.

As I (Brian) began a new teaching assignment as a middle school digital innovations specialist in 2016, I also was granted an incredible opportunity to be a part of the Google Certified Innovator Program. This led to my headfirst dive into the world of creating and playing breakout and puzzle games with my classes. Not long after accepting my place in the program, a strange package arrived. It was a small wooden box with an Innovator logo on it. Inside there were a few random objects. Thirty-six such boxes were sent around the world to all of the members of our cohort. We were given no additional instructions, just boxes and random items. I found that not only was I engaged in an attempt to solve this mystery, but we also were able to develop relationships and understand one another on a deeper level. Since then, I have been using my own creations for digital, physical, and hybrid escape/puzzle style games with incredible success within the classroom. I have worked with various platforms, materials, and concepts to create games accessible for all levels, from the most basic physical games to an impossible game of Clue using CoSpaces Edu to create the experience in virtual reality. No matter where you are in your experience with creating puzzles and games in your classroom, you can find amazing opportunities to engage kids in learning.

In addition to building custom games for my own classes and the teachers with whom I work, I also create and share various free games with the public. Over the past three years, I have had the fortune to write, teach, and demonstrate breakout game concepts for thousands of people. I hope that through sharing our joint knowledge and experiences, Kristen and I will make it easier for everyone to create their own meaningful, engaging experiences.

Preview of book chapter subtopics:

- Cognitive Learning - A pedagogical approach to using breakout boxes and digital breakouts, giving students the opportunity to be effectively engaged in their own learning process. Students will utilize the skills they already have as they enhance their intrapersonal skills, which leads to metacognitive learning.

- Team Building (Collaboration) - Communication is key between participants as they work together to solve clues. Team building will help students learn how to choose roles within the group. Communication also helps with listening skills - to understand each other; develop social skills.

- Enhance Critical Thinking Skills - be able to analyze clues; use prior knowledge to connect and solve. Understanding of right and wrong answers. Being a critical observer - look around the room, notice changes around the room to observe clues. Learn how to share information. Problem-solving skills connect with critical thinking as students will need to identify the problem (clue) and critically think about how to solve it.

- Comprehension - students will be able to retain the information learned better by understanding the content better. Students will be able to work together through collaboration and discussion to solve many clues that lead to a combination of the locks.

- Behavioral Issues - Motivation is an important aspect to get students involved who typically are not involved. We find that curiosity about what's in the box often connects with students who may have social issues. They tend to start slow with participation but realize they can participate in the activity.

"WE ESCAPED"

In a cramped classroom, serving as the Digital Innovations Specialist in my new district, I (Brian) desperately hoped to build the trust of my colleagues and their students. I have found one teacher so far willing to let me try my crazy ideas out with their students. Mrs. Andrea Krier, an 8th-grade science teacher, let me try a few ideas in her classes that most people did not. With that little bit of trust, I pushed the boundary at our school and built my first digital breakout game. Minty Method Madness was created as a series of locked forms with links and references directly back to the study guides and information found in her references for the students. In hindsight, the game was poorly-designed, the puzzles were simplistic, and it lacked anything special about it at all. Except, for the students, it offered more.

> **Minty Method Madness**
>
> The Breakout form for 8th Grade Scientific Method
>
> To find the mints, you need to cycle through. Observe everything, it's information for you. Experiment to test and you'll find interesting things, add what you noticed and find breath that sings.
>
> 3 Digit Code
>
> *Short answer text*
>
> After section 1   Continue to next section

Figure 1.1 - Minty Method Madness

(The above image is the original form for Brian's first Digital Breakout Game)

This first digital breakout game challenged the class in new ways. It required them to look at and think more deeply about the content they were reading through and talk about it together. This visually and systematically bland game was the first I had played with any of the students I worked with, and they loved it. One of the biggest reasons the kids loved working on this was the challenge and satisfaction of solving the clues. The excitement of success and sharing that excitement with teammates within small groups was easily heard throughout the class. It was created as a hybrid game where the final clue at the end of the locked form allowed them to open a single lock that kept a toolbox closed that I had, and still incorporate into some games today. Inside the toolbox, the mints were stolen, and they had thwarted the story's villain using the Scientific Method. I have since revised that game and built many more with increasing degrees of complexity and using various tools. That first game, however, and the trust that Mrs. Krier and her students placed in me allowed me to expand on this for several years to come. Now, Breakout EDU kits and various games are used in our school by multiple teachers and are also used by students who create games for their classes.

From the spark of the original game and the variety of games and uses found by teachers within my school, I found myself creating content to share with others. Over the past several years, I have had the opportunity to develop physical games, including several for Edcamps that led to a great connection between the Edcamp Foundation and Breakout Edu. I have also created many open-source digital games that have allowed thousands of educators and students to access and experience digital breakout and escape room-style games for themselves. Using these experiences in my classroom has helped my students build engagement and demonstrate leadership, learning, and skill sets that do not always present themselves in a traditional classroom.

Maggie Maslowski, a secondary education English teacher, and I collaborated on a breakout box to do together. This would be a difficult challenge for both Maggie and me, as each of us have thirty students in one class, totaling about 60 students per class period. Creating a set of breakout boxes to connect different novels to a dystopian world was challenging enough, let alone ensuring that all the students are actively engaged in the activity. Maggie's sophomore classes read the book *Anthem* by Ann Rand, while my classes read *1984* by George Orwell. Before the activity, we combined students from each of the classes to work together.

With digital breakouts being relatively new to my (Kristen) district, I focused on using the physical breakout game but included the use of technology to solve some of the clues. It was amazing to watch the students collaborate. It was challenging to say the least because the students had to rely on each other. The most challenging part was not to create five different boxes with five sets of combinations but to connect them to two separate novels. For the lesson to work, we needed to collaborate, focusing on the main ideas for each box. Because this was our first attempt at creating our own breakout box, the clues were less complicated. The clues were not supposed to be difficult to solve but was for students to collaborate. This particular breakout box focused on reading two different novels with two different authors. Groups of students were combined from each class to complete the tasks. In order for this to happen, students needed to learn about the novel from the other class.

From creating my first breakout activity, I was hooked on adding gamification into my lessons. I have to admit that I spent more time than I should on creating and visualizing the purpose and the outcome of this activity. But, in the end, it was worth it. No matter how many times I have to redo the clues and combinations to the locks, when my students work together, that inspires me to continue creating this type of activity.

Since then, I have collaborated outside of my district to work with other educators. Most recently, I collaborated with Erin Mueller, a high school teacher at a private high school in Illinois, who was reading the same novel as my classes. To create more authenticity, she visited my class twice. The first time she visited was as a guest speaker teaching the novel from her perspective; the second time she came back to the school to witness the students completing the breakout boxes. She was excited to be a part of a co-collaboration to see how it all worked out. This simple connection with another educator inspired us to learn from each other. She couldn't wait to try it on her students. She then borrowed the boxes for her students to see how well they did against my students. Erin and I discussed how the activity went and made the changes as we saw that was needed.

CROSS-CURRICULAR WORK

Breakouts for Different Purposes

Breakout games can be used in various ways to enhance engagement and interaction with content at various points throughout a unit. While the most common case we see is a review of a topic, these games are versatile enough to engage students at any point in the learning cycle. This section will take a look at examples for using this learning tool at various points of instruction.

Introduction: Introducing a lesson with a breakout is an excellent hook for getting kids excited about a topic. Rather than taking a deep dive into content with this type of game, you provide students with a broader overview of the topic. When creating an introduction, I (Brian) tend to put something we will use during the unit into the box to be opened. One such example is a breakout game I created for my Introduction to Computer Principles course. (See appendix for a link to all the materials for this game.) At the beginning of the section on coding and robotics, I have students work on a breakout that involves some key vocabulary terms, a historical overview of computer science, and essential concepts to coding and robotics without requiring them to fully understand everything they see. Each clue is something I can refer back to during the unit as an example. Inside the box are the Ozobots and markers they will use in the next lesson. If they open the box early, they get to explore the materials until we stop to reflect on the game. This type of game allows students to build excitement for the upcoming content and gives me reference points during future lessons to help students understand the concepts we work through in class.

Formative Assessments: When it's time to gauge which students seem to understand the lesson in your class, a breakout game can be a fun change of pace that will engage them in the work long enough for you to evaluate what your students know. These types of games include various levels of content throughout the experience. While the game itself isn't necessarily the assessment, the content being explored and understood as part of the game creates a perfect opportunity for the teacher to assess what students know and where they still find struggles. One example of a game that provides excellent formative assessment is a hybrid game I created called Fractured Fractions. (See appendix for a link to this game.) In this game, students engage in various online activities that include about a dozen modified questions from a quiz on fractions. During the actual classroom integration of this game, we were able to walk around and get a feel for those who struggled with specific skill sets that were going to be formally assessed shortly.

Review: Whether you are preparing for a significant project or bringing a unit to a close, Breakout games are a great way to build engagement in the class. While I had created several games for teachers looking to review content before an end-of-unit assessment, one of the most memorable experiences was creating a game that paired with a project the following two days. This was an expanded but refined version of the game *Minty Method Madness* (a link to this game is in the appendix), which was the first I had built. In this new game, students continued to learn about and review the Scientific Method. They did so through various means and the inclusion of notes and review presentations shared with the students. After completing the game, the next two class periods involved the students creating their experiment that would follow the steps of the scientific method. When I presented the project alongside the teacher, the student response was precisely what I was hoping to see. Many students had light bulb moments that had, as one kid said, "tricked them into reading over all the details of the scientific method ten times each yesterday." Using the game as a review, students were more confident about the information they needed to access to complete the project. By utilizing a breakout game as a review, this allows for improved retention of content and entices your students to spend more time closely evaluating the information you present to them.

In all of these examples of using Breakout games at various points within a unit, there are a few key things to consider. First, how much content is being infused into the game itself? If you are building a game that is focused on content through this medium, you will want to make as much of the materials as accessible as possible. Rather than hide key components in hard-to-discover places, focus on making the ability to decipher the clues more challenging while ensuring that every group has an opportunity to spend time with the materials. Also, if you want to dive deep into your content, it might make more sense to play the game as a review or preview of a project. If you want to tease the content and create a sense of anticipation for the upcoming unit, then creating the game as a preview makes more sense. Regardless, each of these games is an example of how to use Breakout games at various points in a unit of study to increase engagement with content, collaboration, and critical thinking skills.

How these Concepts Work for any Subject

Creating an interdisciplinary unit using breakout boxes is easier than many think. The difficulty of breakout boxes ranges in difficulty based on how much work you put into it. There are several questions to consider when creating a lesson:

1. What is the lesson that the students should learn before, during, and after the activity?
2. How many breakout boxes will you need for the lesson to be a success?
3. Are you going to create one set (or multiple sets) of directions, combinations for the locks, and/or clues?
4. Are you grouping the students, or will this be a class activity where collaboration is needed to solve the clues?
5. Will there be stations set up around the classroom for students? How will these stations be incorporated into the planning of the unit?

There are a lot of different aspects to think about when creating your breakout activity. To help you get started, there are a few steps to help you in the process of creating your breakout box format (or help you create more difficult challenges for your students if you are not a beginner). You can make it as difficult or easy as you want, depending on the number of boxes, locks, and/or clues. For a beginner, it would be beneficial to create one box to open while leaving clues around the classroom for students to find or create several boxes with the same clues and combinations. This will allow you to refine it later for future classes. Additionally, you may want to leave clues out in the open, so students are not opening up cabinets or drawers in the classroom. Even if you are not a beginner, you can still leave clues for the students to find easily; it does not mean that they will be easily solved.

Various websites can offer help, suggestions, and ideas on creating breakouts for the classroom. Throughout this book, we will list different sites that can be helpful as you create your first or tenth breakout box. If you have a smaller classroom of students, you can create an "escape classroom" instead of using boxes. This will create an opportunity for the students to collaborate instead of competing against each other. Students work together to solve the clues; thus, they will get a better understanding of collaboration and teamwork.

We believe these are the essential skills needed that students can build upon and lead to other skills. Games are created for all ages and all levels of education. Breakout boxes can be aligned to ISTE standards, Common Core State Standards (CCSS), content standards, and even soft learning skills, including the four C's (Critical Thinking, Collaboration, Creativity, and Communication). However, before beginning any breakout game, teachers should discuss the standards and goals with their students so they will have an understanding of what to learn throughout the process. Here are a few steps to help you get started whether you are new to creating breakout boxes or have been doing it for years:

Step 1:

It's important to reflect before creating a game; *what are the goals of the lesson?* Think about the tasks you want to accomplish; what is it that your students want to learn? Are you using this as an introduction to a unit? If this is a formative activity, is this an opportunity to review before a summative assessment? Are you creating a fun game to help the learning process continue throughout the year?

These questions will guide you in creating and setting up your room. Once students are aware that they should be looking at everything, block off classroom areas that are "off-limits" in a physical breakout. Depending on the classroom layout or size, it's possible to create a space just for the game. This alleviates any misdirection or confusion of where students can search for clues.

Step 2:

It's best to focus on what units you can connect to your lesson plans. After reading a novel, it is easy to find a way to connect historical references to a class.

I (Kristen) incorporated meaningful crossover points in solving clues. It isn't difficult to bring in math, geography, grammar, scientific equations, or literacy skills as part of the clues and ciphers used to create and ultimately solve puzzles related to various locks. I incorporated a math equation for students to complete to find and solve one of the lock combinations. I have even used letters from the alphabet where each letter matched a number. For instance. $A = 1$, $B = 2$ and so on. Make sure there are the right number of letters to numbers. This creates the critical thinking skills needed to solve harder problems.

It is easy to find crossover points. Curriculum frequently lends itself to activities that build upon multiple subject areas at once. It can even be possible to work with other staff members and have games that continue from one class to another.

Step 3:

Find similarities between the course you are teaching to the course(s) with which you want to connect. It's best to think about your current course and begin building out using courses you are familiar with. This can be a collaboration with colleagues or even your students. Just remember to focus on one or two courses when designing your breakout box. Too many may alter the goal(s) of the lesson. It doesn't mean that it's not possible to do this later.

Step 4:

Identify what materials you have available. This doesn't just mean locks, kits, and tools that are used for the actual escape room or breakout game, but also, and perhaps, more importantly, what resources will help the students achieve success. One of the best things about creating breakout games is how students access and assess learning resources. Knowing the resources the students will access and the resources you have at hand to create the game will allow you to plan both the box and the scenarios.

Step 5:

Begin planning your breakout box. Before working out the locks and scenarios, start brainstorming ideas. If you have more than one class that will use the box(es), it's best to time how long it will take to reset each box. You can also have students reset the boxes before the end of the class. Next, create scenarios for students to read, watch, or play with clues to help them find additional clues to solve or locate the combinations to the locks. Before testing it on the students, go through the clues and the combinations yourself, or if possible, have a partner/coworker test it out for you. It's easy to make a mistake when setting up more than one or multiple boxes.

Ways to Connect Curriculum within Games

As stated earlier, before connecting your course with other courses, you will need to find the similarities between them. Typically this is not the time to introduce any new material that has not been taught or covered, but we will discuss games as introductions later in the book. The purpose of this type of breakout box is to review lessons that were previously taught.

English is an easy place to start for crossover into various curriculum topics. For additional ways to create breakout activities, visit: https://kristenkoppers.wixsite.com/diteaching/breakout-boxes.

COGNITIVE LEARNING BY ENGAGING STUDENTS

Engaging Students in Learning:
Aubrey Yeh EscapED

Although I have run several Breakout EDU games myself, one of my favorite experiences was stepping into another school as an observer. In this K-8 school, small groups of middle school students were given the assignment of creating a game for a certain grade level of elementary students at their school, which they subsequently were able to run with the students. When I heard about this, I knew I wanted to see how it turned out!

I walked into the library on the day of the game and watched as the middle schoolers explained the scenario to the elementary schoolers and started the timer. As I watched, I was amazed at the quality of the clues - they looked like they were designed by a teacher, not a student just a few years older. As I talked to the game designers, they shared that as a part of this project, they met with the elementary teachers during their planning period to learn exactly which skills the students were working on at the time. They divided up the subject areas, so one group member made a clue involving math (fractions), one created a social studies-focused clue (map-reading), and so on. They then came together to create a cohesive story that tied it all together.

While it was fun watching the elementary students work on the clues and apply their learning, what has stuck with me is how much the middle school students must have learned from this experience. They had to think like teachers about learning, create clues at the students' skill level that was engaging, and collaborate on a final product. This meta-cognition of the learning process extends beyond one game, and I heard them incorporating these new understandings into their learning process as they reflected. At the end of the day, one group of students was able to review content in a fun and engaging way, another group was able to think deeply about the learning process, and ALL of them walked away with a sense of accomplishment and pride!

Cognitive learning is a pedagogical approach that can be applied to using breakout boxes by allowing students to be effectively engaged in their own learning process. Students will be actively engaged in their learning, especially through collaboration. Benjamin Bloom created a hierarchy of "needs" based on higher thinking skills.

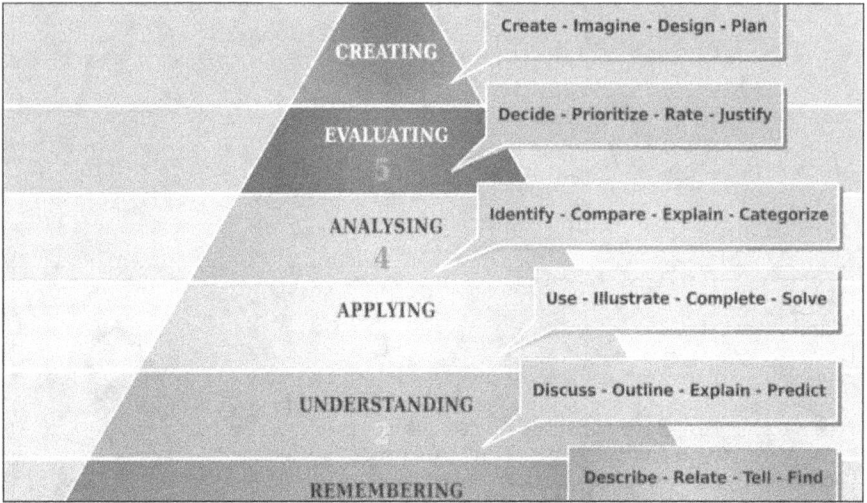

Figure 3.1 - Bloom's Taxonomy of higher thinking.

To move from one level to the next, students do not have to master each level; instead, they need to reach a level to show success in their performance by completing certain objectives.

The first level of the cognitive domain focuses on remembering where basic facts are recalled from the lessons. While using breakout boxes, students will focus on recalling specific ideas, events, defining certain terms, or memorizing significant characters, formulas, dates, and other concepts. Since this is the first domain of the hierarchy, students will need to demonstrate this level before moving onto the next. However, even if the students can demonstrate the knowledge of the first level, it does not necessarily mean that they omit the facts. This level is the beginning of recalling information.

The second level is crucial as it begins with higher-level thinking skills of understanding certain concepts or ideas. At this level, students will need to explain their reasoning for solving clues. They will also need to discuss, through collaboration, how one clue leads to another. Students, at this level, will need to categorize information and be able to discuss it within their group. Instead of just repeating facts, ideas, or information, students will focus more on defending their decisions. While this is not an intricate part of the process, they use the critical thinking skills needed to move to level three.

The third level of Bloom's revised Taxonomy is the application of information as students respond to the clues. They will apply what they learned throughout the game and connect their learning to prior knowledge. At this level, students use complex clues to solve problems. However, some clues may be more difficult than others.

The fourth level is to learn how to analyze by breaking apart the information or purely focusing on one part of the clue to conclude. Throughout the analysis process, students are challenged to a higher level of thinking. This is part of the deconstruction process where some clues are directly stated while others are not. This means that students at this level learn how to read the clues but look for other hints or additional clues within a single clue. This extends with higher thinking skills by drawing additional connections.

The fifth level is where students evaluate the information they are given during the game. At this level, students use their problem-solution process with the clues to critically think "outside the box," as some clues are more difficult than others. Part of the evaluation process in a breakout game is connecting one clue to others. It is possible to have one clue lead to another before students figure out the clue for a combination or key lock. While the previous levels focus more during the game, the last two levels are more for the small or large group discussion afterward as students reflect on their progress.

The last and final level of the cognitive domain is the creation process. This is often thought to be a structural part of the breakout lesson. For students to solve the clues at this level, their critical thinking skills are at a higher level by hypothesizing the progression of the clues. Depending on how you construct your breakout game, students may have all the clues at once and will need to decide which clue is essential to solve first. If a higher level clue is solved first, it would open a lock or prevent students from solving the lower level clues.

When creating a breakout game, each clue can be created around the six levels of Bloom's Taxonomy. This will allow students to answer clues at different learning levels. The first clue will be geared towards level one, where students will recall, memorize, or define certain pieces of information before moving to the second clue giving students the ability to discuss with their group members possible solutions to the clue. The teacher will create six clues moving up the pyramid of Bloom's Taxonomy.

When teachers use Bloom's Taxonomy in a breakout game, it allows students to learn as they actively solve the clues. Remember, it's all about the different ways to support students in their learning.

COLLABORATION LEADS TO TEAM BUILDING AND COMMUNICATION

I n my (Kristen) book, *Differentiated Instruction in the Teaching Profession*, a chapter focuses on learning how to collaborate with colleagues. Just as educators collaborate to create a team-building exercise, students will be able to follow their lead by communicating with classmates. Collaboration goes a long way when students can tackle challenging tasks and questions. There are three specific ways that student collaboration will increase success: creating a sense of ownership through engagement, learning to use problem-solving skills in difficult situations, and focusing on students' intrapersonal skills to lead to interpersonal skills effectively. Ultimately, they will feel a sense of accomplishment. But it's important to note that collaboration among students cannot be forced.

Student collaboration on a breakout box lesson depends on the teacher. There have been teachers that created breakout boxes early on in the school year and some towards the end of the semester. Either way, as a teacher, you know your students; it is a good idea to create small group discussions before attempting the breakout lesson, as they are designed to build collaboration among students and enhance their communication skills.

If the students cannot complete all the tasks within the given amount of time, they should understand what caused them difficulties. Ask them where problems arose, so the process can be changed to achieve success next time. Student ownership in the activity is equally as important as being successful.

Student Success through Engagement

We all know that attempting to engage students of any age can be challenging at times. The elementary students all want to shout out answers to the question, while the secondary education students don't even think about raising their hands to answer a question. And then we've seen everything in between. The importance of creating a sense of ownership through engagement increases student motivation. The way a breakout box activity creates student engagement is through teamwork. By waiting until the day of the lesson to create groups, it invokes a rivalry between friends. We all want students to take ownership of their learning, and you know your students best. Just remember, there are students who may not speak out or join a group on their own. Pre-decided groups take away from the alienation of excluding certain students in a class.

Student success through engagement comes from collaboration and teamwork. Breakout EDU will transform students from individual thinkers to collaborative learners. "This is where Breakout EDU comes in. Breakout EDU is an immersive learning game platform where players use teamwork and critical thinking to solve a series of challenging puzzles to open a locked box" (Romano-Arrabito, 2017). From personal experiences, we have seen students overcome challenges to solve a series of clues.

We've seen students who were not defeated, even if they weren't successful in breaking out. They were able to do so by focusing on their reflections. Students were given time to go back through and recall their steps to understand if there was a better way to solve the clues or open the locks. Even though the game was officially over when the time counted to 0:00, students were still engaged in the lesson. The ultimate goal of the breakout boxes is not for teachers to create a gamified activity just to keep students engaged, but rather to allow students to be engaged in the learning process.

Learning How to Use Problem-Solving Skills

A social skill that students need to achieve before graduating high school is learning how to problem-solve complex issues. While students will learn how to problem-solve throughout school, many are not given a chance to think critically outside the classroom. This is where breakout boxes help students develop their skills in critical thinking as they learn how to think about their reasoning. Part of critical thinking skills is to reflect upon decisions, which improves learning by questioning decisions and rethinking possible strategies.

The best part of creating or using a breakout activity is that teachers can make it as easy or hard as they want to for students to think critically. (This will be discussed in more detail in chapter 6.) As mentioned earlier, teachers create breakout boxes based on the intended goal. For example, teachers created breakout boxes for a Forensic Science class where students solved a crime scene investigation. Likewise, elementary school students learned about history when the United States Constitution was stolen. Students first figure out which clue they need to solve first. There might be a particular order students need to solve the clues to "win" the game, which is why problem-solving skills are essential. During a breakout activity, I (Kristen) labeled the cards 1 - 5. The cards all had different clues that led students to additional clues or the combinations to locks. However, the activity sheet students were to complete had to be completed in a specific order (hence the numbers 1 - 5). Students who successfully opened all the locks but did not write the answers down in the correct order had to go back through to determine the order the locks were opened to complete the activity.

Problem-solving skills are not just used during the activity, but are also used from when the students walk into the classroom until the time they leave.

Student excitement and engagement generate a sense of urgency around the problem. Most players quickly identify that if they can work together, split up tasks, and collaborate on clues that they will be more successful. With the desire to solve challenges and clues increasing as students unlock each lock on the box, the motivation to find new and efficient ways to collaborate can become very impressive. In one breakout game, I (Brian) played with a 6th-grade computer principles class, I watched five girls who spoke four different languages among them find ways to collaborate and complete their breakout challenge. I admit to being concerned at first, knowing the group would have to overcome their significant language barrier to be successful. Not only were they successful, but they were also able to complete their challenge before the other team in the class. This is just one of the many powerful examples of how our students can use their motivation and engagement to promote powerful collaboration.

Using Intrapersonal Skills to Form Interpersonal Skills

While creating and using breakout boxes, it's important to think about the relationships between the teacher and students and their peers as there may be some extroverts, who do not need the encouragement to participate, and introverts who might need a little help collaborating with their peers. This leads to some students who enjoy participating during class while some do not want any type of 'attention' in a group setting. The best way to encourage all students to participate is to have a mixture of clues to solve (ones that might need one person to solve and others that would require a few students to work together).

Students who are introverts are sometimes believed to be not overly concerned about their feelings, which can be viewed negatively as introverts may appear to only think about themselves. Educationally speaking, this is far from the truth. It can be said that introverts are concerned for their feelings but only based on feeling neglected or excluded from a group. An introvert may not participate in a discussion for fear of being ridiculed by their classmates. In contrast, an extrovert is more of an outgoing person who readily engages in discussions. However, there are times that "extroverts are easy for introverts to understand, because extroverts spend so much of their time working out who they are in voluble, and frequently inescapable, interaction with other people" (Rauch, 2003). The distinction between the two relies heavily on the interaction not only with the teacher but peers too. Ultimately, this leads to the fact that a student's self-esteem is based on one's intrapersonal skills. Students may think about solutions in their heads while others can talk out loud to form connections. Even though one is internally thought about and the other is spoken, both are considered intrapersonal skills. Students who are introverts may also have difficulty expressing their intrapersonal thoughts clearly and logically to their classmates, thus why group collaboration is an intricate component to breakout lessons/activities. "Introverts desire to be understood but often lack the ability to speak up, sharing their impressions, thoughts and connections" (Harrington-Atkinson, 2017). They will figure out things and process them entirely before talking and sharing what they know. Combining introverts and extroverts in one group will help those students who battle with their intrapersonal and interpersonal skills.

Students who are extroverts are sometimes better with certain aspects of interpersonal skills, as they could be more likely to speak freely while interacting with classmates. Breakout lessons and activities connect students who are introverts and extroverts together by sharing a common goal. "In our extrovertist society, being outgoing is considered normal and therefore desirable, a mark of happiness, confidence, leadership" (Rauch, 2003). Students who are introverts, and those who are extroverts, can support each other in this gamified situation.

The Opportunity to Enhance Critical Thinking Skills

As mentioned earlier, critical thinking is one of the soft skills students need to learn in school. Students often believe that the first one to complete the activity wins the game. Unfortunately, this is far from the truth. We are used to playing board games where each player chooses a token and moves the piece to a certain number of places. Similarly, when playing a game, the one who scores the most points (or lowest in golf) wins. The problem with this type of 'win' is that there is not much critical thinking taking place. It's easy to move a piece around the board or (if you are good enough) to hit a ball across a green to score points. Where students learn critical thinking skills is in the classroom when there is not a board to move around, no dice to be rolled, or even a green to play on. Critical thinking skills cannot be found in a box but rather working together to solve clues to find the right combinations for the 'win.'

COMPREHENSION THROUGH COGNITIVE LEARNING

Comprehension is an important part of cognitive learning as it develops students' knowledge and enhances their skills to become better readers. But comprehension is not only used for reading; it is needed to understand mathematical equations, historical connections, and making inferences in science. The ability for students to comprehend certain types of information actively engages them to increase learning. No matter what the lesson's objectives are or how much we want the students to learn, cognitive learning comes from intentional and unintentional learning. Students focus on what they have already learned (prior knowledge), connecting it to the new information.

How does comprehension help students in gamification? Gamification is a simple aspect of a game that involves using critical thinking skills to encourage engagement in the classroom. Gamification is not creating a game, but using existing components of game mechanics to engage learning. Memory is an essential part of engaging learning as it is necessary to recall information for specific purposes.

During one of the Breakout sessions conducted in a secondary education English classroom, students needed to recall information said in class as well as written notes to solve the clues throughout the game. Those who were not actively engaged or could not comprehend the material had difficulty participating in their group. As teachers, we can enhance those skills the students already possess. Cognitive learning is not about memorizing information from a text to recall it later. Cognitive learning uses a student's knowledge to focus on the deeper meaning to form conclusions through logical thinking.

Through the game format, student comprehension is increased, not simply by playing, but because of the attention and repeated exposure to the content. Just as mentioned in the previous paragraph, it is not about memorizing the content but learning through skills needed to process the information. Students don't build a stronger understanding of the material because they are playing a game, but because they spend more time actively engaged in the material. In the game mentioned in Section 1 of this book, Minty Method Madness, the students worked through multiple aspects of the scientific method within the digital breakout. The following day they had to do a project that incorporated the scientific method. They commented on how easy it was to work through the steps of the project. At that point, they were let in on the secret that they had been tricked into reading, watching, and examining material that prepared them for the project several times the previous day.

Remember, cognitive learning is not about memorization, but rather how to enhance the skills needed from previous learning information. Using the Breakout games as a gamification method for teaching content provides an excellent opportunity for a deeper comprehension of the material. While it should not be the only method for students to learn and build an understanding of new materials, it is a handy tool in introducing, reviewing, and expanding learning and comprehension for your students.

CREATING YOUR OWN GAMES

Whether you're building a physical breakout or going digital, there needs to be a scenario in the introduction. The teacher can create the scenario, or it can be taken from a previous lesson. For instance, students in Kristen's class learned about dystopian literature while reading George Orwell's novel *1984*. The scenario was based on key points from the book. Using these types of scenarios will help students understand the goal of the lesson and get them started on the clues. To create your breakout box, think about a game board. Each game board has certain pieces related to the game, the game board itself, and instructions on how to play. This is the same for breakout boxes. Each breakout game will have certain locks, different boxes, and the scenario to begin the game. Throughout the game, there will be additional clues to help students throughout the lesson. It's not necessary to have all the clues given to the students at once.

For my (Kristen) breakout boxes, I like to be creative in how I set them up. Besides changing the lock combinations for all locks, I include material to get the students to think, "why is this here?" For example, after reading the novel, Slaughterhouse Five by Kurt Vonnegut, the timeline of events that occurred throughout the novel were important. Each pack contained 4 playing cards that mimicked the year to the clue on the envelope. The students were able to use their notes, recall information from the novel, or even use the backboard with the timeline to help solve this clue.

After participating in several escape rooms, I modified the ways clues were created and how to set up the boxes for the classroom. The use of magazines and books placed around the room or close to the breakout boxes creates suspense in thinking, 'why are they here?' Another type of puzzle to let students solve is highlighting certain words in books. Most 'resources' that are used have a clue to connect it to. The clue can give a specific page number to turn to with another clue or the answer to a lock combination. Each breakout game can be as creative as you want it to be. A recent breakout game consisted of codes and red herrings that were not part of the activity.

In planning my (Brian) breakout games, I let the theme tell the story. Whatever the breakout is about, I build a storyline around it. While creating a breakout about code breaking in WWII, the game was themed around solving an important encrypted message while working with the famous Alan Turing. In creating a different breakout about the Revolution, the theme centered around a messenger Thaddeus Bowman and how you can help him deliver a crucial warning to the Colonists' Captain.

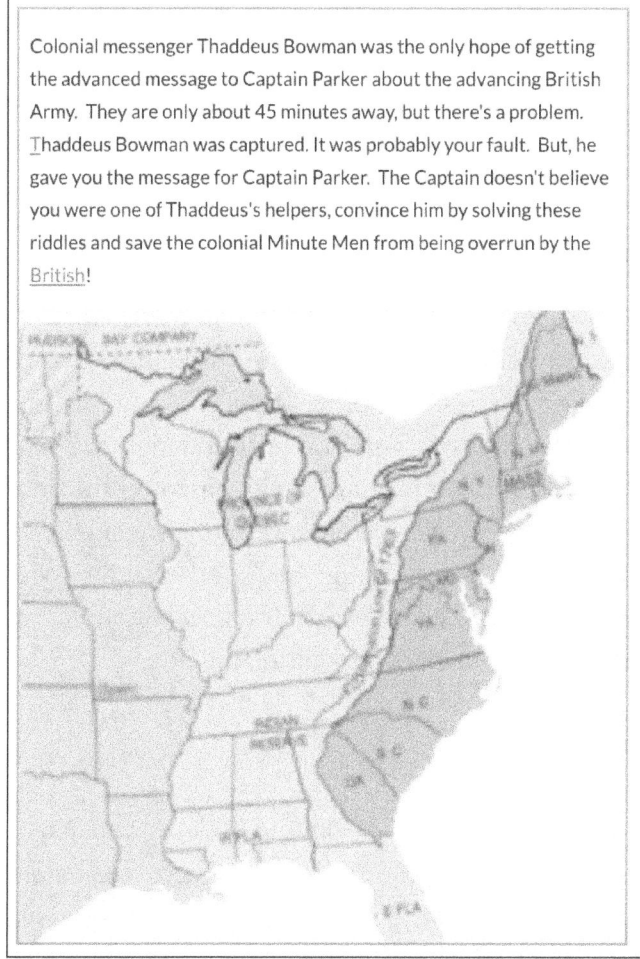

Although the story can pull your students into the game, I have found that the better the puzzles for each lock, the greater the student engagement. Unless I have a particular storyline that inspires me to create a game, I start with the same principles as any quality lesson design.

My first step is to identify what the purpose of my game will be. What do I want my kids to take away or learn from this? From there, I start identifying key questions that can help them to reach the goals

I have for their learning. Next, I identify my resources. Whether I am creating a digital game, a hybrid game, or a physical box, it's about knowing what my students will access to identify concepts or learn changes how the game is designed. Whether you have articles, book passages, magazines, images, maps, videos, audio files, or anything else, the materials students access dramatically impact what they learn and retain while playing the game. Not only are the resources your students access for learning meaningful in shaping the game, but they are also the resources you have to build it. The number of boxes, kits, locks, devices, and other supplies per student can significantly change the kind of game you should design. It's important to remember to design the breakout activity based on the knowledge of your students. As my students were aware of my thinking, they were focusing on thinking "outside the box" rather than trying to find literal answers. This method is continuously used in my classes, which results in students thinking outside the box.

Creating Your Breakout Lessons

With all the different sources on the web and teachers sharing breakout templates, a question arises: "if there are others creating breakout lessons online, why should I do it?" We've been asked this a lot. It's easy to share ideas with fellow educators instead of creating your own game. The problem that we ran into was that the focus of some of the other games did not meet the needs of what the students were learning. Although there are many great games available, it can be incredibly powerful to have games explicitly created with your own students in mind. When we start using these games as introductions to units, reviews, and formative assessments of general understanding, we will usually need a more sophisticated tool. Think of it this way: would sharing a unit test over the novel be the same for every teacher? While we think that there would not be a difference, what we teach is different for every class and every teacher. Sharing is a great way to learn from each other and focus on being innovative educators. By creating your breakout lesson, you will be able to customize your lesson to use as a review or formative assignment.

When completing your breakout box, it's a good idea to create a *Doc, Spreadsheet, Presentation, or Web* (see appendix for examples) for a place to keep the clues and lock combinations. It's also an easy place to share information with other educators. Additionally, *Google* Docs and *Google* Forms automatically save the work as it's created, which is beneficial in case you want to share your work with others by showing a view-only format.

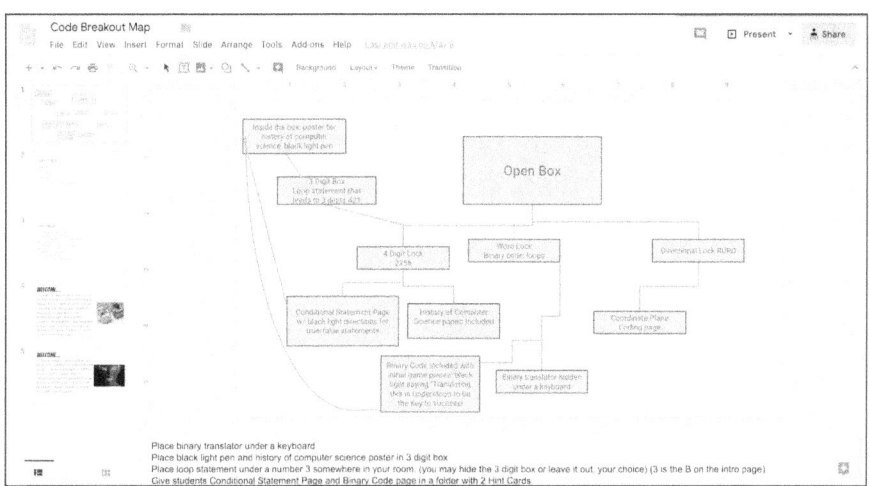

Figure 6.1 shows how each puzzle is planned and connected. It also includes the solutions to each.

Building games has always seemed a daunting task for most educators with whom we work. Seeing the finished product of a complex, well-connected game that an experienced user has created can look incredibly overwhelming. What we've found is that for many students, even simpler, more straightforward games are significantly engaging and offer challenge and interest. As you grow into your style and game development, your students will grow with you. Don't be afraid to challenge yourself or your students. If the game is created as a win or lose situation, students will negatively approach completing any future breakout activities.

Rather than set those complex games as your guiding star, focus on designing an effective lesson. Start as you would any lesson, with something you want your students to learn or understand.

Once you have a firm idea of what you want your students to know, identify sources of information from which you have pulled that content. Sources could be anything from videos to articles to posters. From there, building the game gets started. Your first game will almost always be a bit rougher around the edges; but what is most intriguing is how your students' ability to solve problems, pull apart puzzles, and connect complex ideas and information will grow as your ability to create more complex games develops. Essentially, we have noticed that our students' ability at problem-solving and collaborating during the game grew alongside our ability to build better puzzles. There were times that clues or combinations were located behind pictures that were never part of the classroom. Students learn the classroom layout, wall decorations, and, essentially, what is 'normally' there and not there. As students get better at identifying things out of place in their surroundings, it can be a useful challenge to begin hiding your items in plain sight. To create a sense of suspense, I (Kristen) will place these items out a few days to a week before using the breakout activity.

As you read through the rest of this section, we will provide you with tools and tricks to advance your puzzle creation, but the essence of the game is still the same. Focus on the learning, provide your students with resources, and then give them some gentle guidance built into the game's clues. If you do that, you will find so many of the incredible positives created using these puzzle-based breakout games.

Offer students clue cards or hints if they are having trouble. Walk around the room and help when needed. Listening to students discuss the strategies to solve the clues is as beneficial to you as a teacher as it is for the students. Because students have different learning abilities, it's essential to understand which clues may be more difficult for students to answer. By understanding this, it will help when revising this activity next time.

Ideas for creating digitally shared strategies for building the game

Unlike the physical breakout boxes where teachers would have different items, such as boxes, locks, paper clues, and UV pens, digital breakout boxes are entirely online, and teachers do not have to purchase items to participate.

Breakout EDU has developed its platform and can be an excellent place to start for beginners, especially if you have access to the platform. Games made on the Breakout EDU website are usually pretty straightforward in design, though that does not mean you cannot create a solid and engaging game. The platform is designed to be an easy way to break into game creation, and an equally easy visual set up for students to play games for the first time.

Breakout EDU's Digital Platform

In October of 2017, Breakout EDU launched its specialized platform for digital Breakout games. This platform was created and brought some uniformity and consistency to digital games. It is a visually appealing and user-friendly platform that provides a level of simplicity that makes each game accessible to anyone using it. One of the most significant benefits of using Breakout EDU's digital platform is that it is user-friendly. Not only is it easy to search for games, play games regardless of what devices or software your school uses, access a rich resource of content-based games, but it is also a great way to launch yourself into starting your game creation. Using the Breakout EDU digital platform practically walks you through the entire process of creating your own game. It provides you with virtual locks and a place to keep all of your information stored. It creates an easy way to engage your students with games in a format that will become quickly recognizable to your students.

Using this can also be an excellent way for your students to start creating games. Because of its simplicity and intuitive nature in matching with the physical breakout games, the transition to creating games leaves your students with only a small leap from solving puzzles to creating them. This single lock example of a game created for demonstration purposes during professional development shows how easy it is to create something complex or confusing in other formats, a color lock.

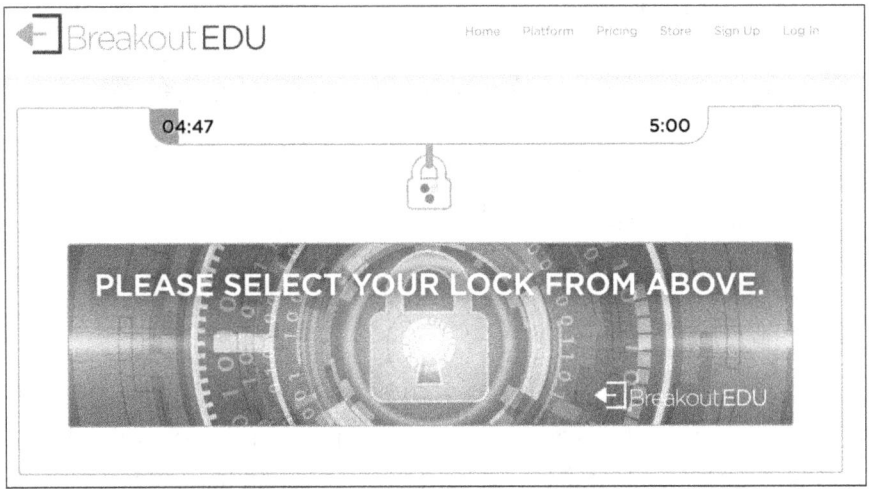

Figure 6.2 - Player's Screen for Breakout Edu Platform

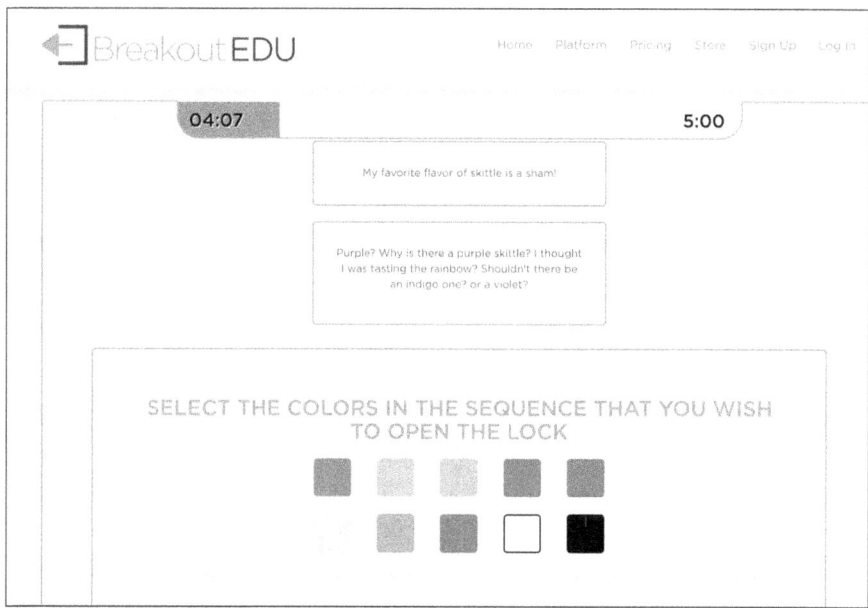

Each lock in the game is under the timer (top). When you click on the lock, you see the clue (bottom).

Using the platform has several advantages for both educators hoping to create the game and students playing. One of the challenges it has in common with creating physical games is that the locks still have some limits. Game creators are still required to translate important concepts acquired from the game in various media into ideas that can equate to a lock. There are many ways to do this. (See our resources in the physical game section.) The need to translate answers into digits, colors, directions, or short letter combinations adds a layer to the game that engages students. It can, however, make matching up important content and the locks different for the game maker.

While this platform has helped bring digital escape room games and Breakout EDU to more people than ever before, there are many ways to create escape room games for your students. If you don't have access to the Breakout EDU Digital platform, or you are looking for ways to expand on games, a Google Form is a great way to create a digital breakout box for students to complete. One way to do this is to have each question or set of questions that can be divided into sections where students need to complete the first question or set of questions before they are allowed to move to the next group. Figure 6.3 on the following page is an example of how to create a Google form for students. You have a choice to have students either answer correctly before moving on to the next clue, or create a form where students have to solve all the clues. It's best to create a form based on the content you are testing, the level of understanding, and/or knowledge for your students.

Dystopian Society

The year is 3032 where World War III was a nuclear war that caused the nation to crumble once again to create a dystopian society. You are the last survivors; you have 45 minutes to breakout to be to be considered safe. If you don't succeed, you will become a casualty of war. There are five boxes. You have been grouped and must work together to survive. You are not safe; inside the locked box your group will find a piece of paper to help you survive until the democratic power is restored. You must work together as a team. There are five locks. However, each lock will have a key or code needed to open it. You must figure out the clues to find the combinations.

Clue 1: The novels, 1984, and Anthem are set in a dystopian society. There are several themes associated with these novels. In order to find the key or combination to a lock, you, you will need to answer the question: The difference in years of the date 1984 was written and the year Anthem was written then double it.

Short answer text

Figure 6.3 is an example of a digital breakout using Google Forms. Students will be required to answer each question correctly before moving on to the next one. Students can solve the clue multiple times if their first answer is incorrect. As a teacher, you can offer a clue to help students solve it with too many wrong answers. Above is an example of a beginner's clue where not much collaboration is needed to start. There are five clues similar to the one shown in figure 6.3. Each clue was specific to a box number. For this particular clue, students would need to read the clue and research the publication date of the two novels. Students had to subtract the years and double the final answer for the combination to the lock. However, not all clues were easy. It's best to have some easier clues, so students do not get discouraged when playing.

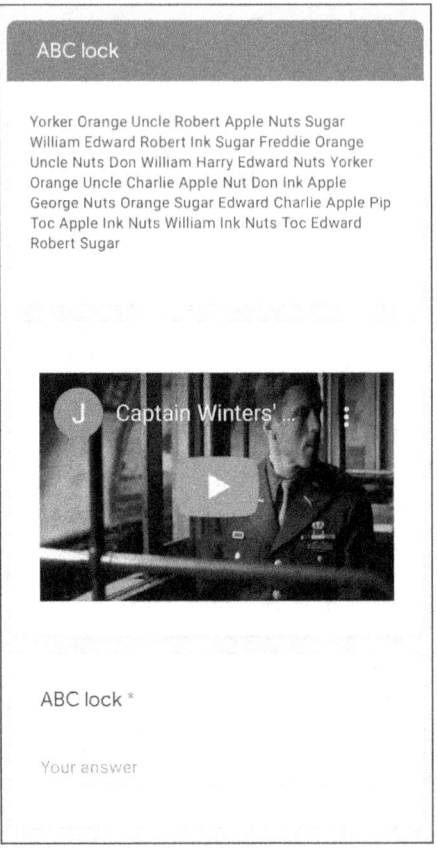

Figure 6.4 is another example of a digital breakout In this breakout, students have to complete the locks with the correct codes in order to continue. The Google Form will not allow a group to continue without the correct code as the clues were sectioned off. This particular question is for the ABC lock, where the students have to use the two clues to figure out the code. A YouTube video was also inserted into the clue to help students solve it.

Another way to create a game using Google Forms is to create an entire set of locks on one form and embed them into a Google Site. You can then add layers to the game by creating a landing site students will access only when they have completed the first form. This is usually how I create a hybrid game. Students will complete the form on the home page of the site while needing a link placed in the completion message of the Google Form that will take them to a final hint that helps them open a physical box. (A link to *Road to the Revolution* can be found in the appendix.)

Figure 6.5 shows a game made in Google Sites, with the home page (top) being the main focus, and a hidden page with a final clue for a physical box (bottom).

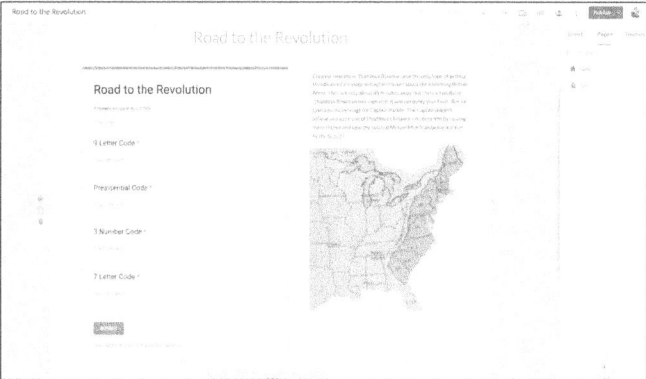

Google Forms are just one of many possible tools that can be intertwined within your breakout games. Edutech tools can also be linked, focusing on a greater way to learn. Technology tools such as Padlet and ThingLink are great tools to use for clues. Students will be able to log into a pre-designed Padlet to solve the clue. To ensure there is no sharing of answers, you can create a Padlet for each group.

Because the ThingLink tool is excellent for adding supplementary material, there is no need to create more than one. Groups will be able to use the information that matches their specific clues. This tool has a picture as a background with points of learning added to it by the teacher. Student signing into the program is not required to access the information. There are countless tools to incorporate into digital games. In addition to the Digital Platform, Google Sites, Google Forms, and ThingLink, I (Brian) have also had success using games that follow a map using Google MyMaps and Google Earth, Slides and PowerPoint, RoundMe, My360.io, and creating games in virtual reality using CoSpaces. The housing for the game is less important than the connection between the content and the resources that your students will be expected to make.

For the digital breakout to be successful, students must have access to an electronic device accessing the internet. It is beneficial to have everyone on their device and collaborate while all have access to the information. Unlike most physical breakout games, it is much easier to create smaller groups or partners to work together. Limiting the number of students working together on a digital breakout will help to ensure that all of your students are engaged and have the opportunity to collaborate and contribute.

In place of physical locks to open, images of open locks can symbolize the achievement once a clue has been solved. This is an added effect to opening a lock. Regardless of how you choose to show students markers of success, the satisfaction of solving puzzles and completing the challenge is ever-present. During one digital breakout game where students were solving math problems, I once had a student shout out "YES!" then broke down in tears. When I went to talk to her, she had told me she was never able to do those math problems before when she did them in class, but she wanted to keep trying to help her team be successful at the game. She was overwhelmed with her sense of accomplishment at finally finding success.

Even with digital breakouts, a digital timer can be projected on a screen to give students a certain amount of time to complete it. The timer is helpful for several reasons. First, it builds a sense of urgency that students have a limited time to complete this activity. It also gives you an idea about how teams are pacing themselves out during the activity. Using a timer can be a good gauge for you if your game is too hard, too easy, or just right. If you are finding teams not solving problems halfway through the entire process, it might be a good idea to nudge them in the right direction. If your game is based on getting your students engaged in the content, not figuring any of the clues out isn't helpful. Often you will find that when you nudge a team in the right direction with a subtle hint or clue, they will suddenly start realizing several things about the game.

Tech Tools to Help Create Digital Breakout Boxes

Thinglink	Padlet	Flipgrid	Snotes
A digital tech tool that uses visual images into an interactive graphic that has embedded information.	An online bulletin board that creates a visual for students. Using Padlet in a breakout box for information, clues, lock combinations, or videos to watch.	An online social platform that is video taped with clues that lead to other clues or the combination to locks.	An online or printable tool that holds secret messages or combinations to locks. Students will need to rotate the image to find all the secret messages hidden within the shape of colors.
Google Maps/Earth	**CoSpaces**	**Slides/Powerpoint**	**RoundMe**
Google Maps and Google Earth Tour Creator can be used to embed clues, text, images, and links into the locations on the map. This can be used as a clue or to house the game overall.	Cospaces is an ARVR creation program that can add an intriguing wrinkle to any game. I have built games where all the clues are within the VR space, physical games where a Merge Cube puzzle holds the clue to open a lock, and also games where a single puzzle is created in VR.	Using presentation software like Slides or Powerpoint, (also Drawing software) allows you to hide links in a picture, create scenes, fake text messages or social media messages, or puzzles within the game.	RoundMe is a program that works like ThingLink except that the images are all 360 degree images. Using RoundMe or other programs like it can work as a way to hide content, or embed links to other puzzles for your game.

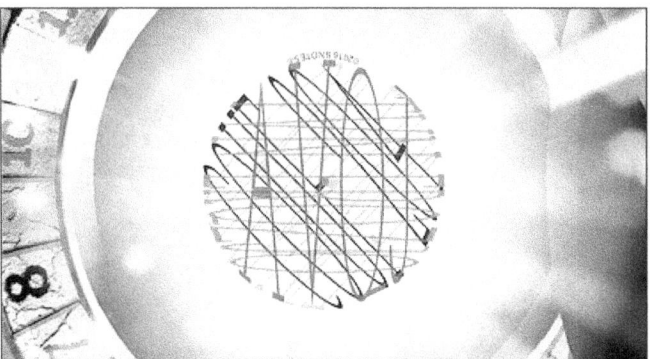

Figure 6.6 - The above image is an example of a Snote clue. Students need to rotate the image on their device or on paper to read hidden messages. They come in all shapes, sizes, and colors. To solve this type of clue, they will need to rotate the image in several directions to read the entire message. You can even change the colors with different words if you like with each rotation. However, even when students are able to find all the words, they will still need to put them in order to solve the clue.

ESCAPE ED   43

Ideas, strategies, and challenges for building physical games

Creating games using your physical box can be both rewarding and challenging, but it does not have to be an overwhelming process. Many games use the materials that come with the Breakout EDU kit and on the accompanying website. The opportunity to play and run a few games from the site is beneficial to build your arsenal of tools. While we will share strategies for creating physical games, there are always new ideas, resources, and unlimited possibilities. The kit (Figure 6.7) comes with everything you need to get started with making engaging and effective games. From there, you will begin to see ways to see many objects in your classroom and your everyday life as part of your puzzles and challenges for students to overcome.

Creating your own breakout lesson(s):

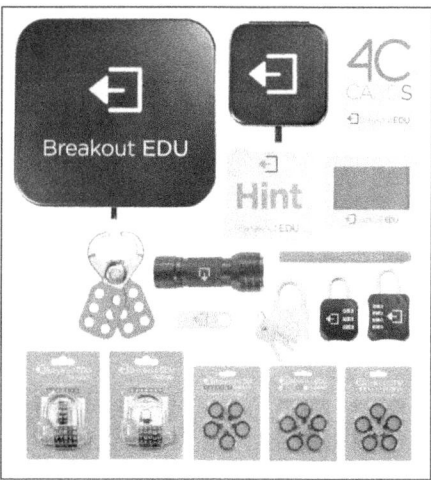

Figure 6.7 - **The official breakout kit (above) can be found on www.breakoutedu.com. It has locks, hasp, four clue cards, hint cards, UV flashlight, USB drive, decoder reader, and the main box. There are ways to add to the box by adding extra locks, different locks, an invisible pen, and more.**

Breakout boxes are easy to create and can cost anywhere from $50 - $150, depending on how many locks and size boxes you will use for the classroom. One complete breakout set can be bought on www.breakout.edu. If you want to create and design your own set of boxes, we listed some items included in a beginner and advanced set of learning. Many of the items listed below are found at the local hardware store, dollar store, or even a grocery store. However, items can vary depending on the goal of the lesson. You may add items at your own discretion.

Beginner:		
4 – digit combination lock (2)	Directional Lock (1)	Smaller toolbox (1)
3 – digit combination lock (2)	UV flashlight (1)	Hasp (1)
Spy pen (1)	Word lock (1)	Large toolbox (1)

Advanced:		
4 – digit combination lock (2)	Books	Wooden Puzzle Box
3 – digit combination lock (3)	Large toolbox (1)	Magazines
Spy pen (1)	Small 3-digit key lock box (1)	Hasp (2)
Individual Scrabble Tiles	UV flashlight (1)	Directional Lock (1)
Pencil bad w/ lock (1)	Locked Diary (1)	Smaller toolbox (1)
"Birthday" Lock (1)	USB flash drive (1)	Hidden Compartment objects around classroom (i.e., clock, fake book, thermometer, etc.)

Building a physical game can be simple or time-consuming, depending on what you want your students to learn. After completing the steps from Chapter 2, it's essential to figure out how many lockboxes (and sizes) are needed, how many different locks you will need, and what the result will be once students have broken into the box. Because Kristen teaches secondary education, she used different approaches for her students to be successful. Working with seniors, the breakout box was used at the end of the semester, where successful students would find an outline of what was on the final writing exam.

To avoid sharing clues and combinations, each box had similar clues with different answers and varying lock combinations. Creating this breakout box took a couple of hours to ensure the clues and combinations matched the correct number box. To ensure the accuracy of the clues and combinations, I double checked all the clues and combinations to ensure they work before using them in the classroom. Because the final exam was the result, each box was created to ensure success. This is another aspect to think about when designing the activities.

Every time I create a breakout box, I like to create new challenges for students. Here are a few ideas that were used in a secondary education English classroom:

Creating stations for students to complete:

Depending on the grade level taught, stations can be set up for each box. Instead of students having the material at the box, stations are set up where students must complete the clues in order. Each station would have an envelope associated with their box number. This can be completed in different ways: have students start at different stations where they can rotate from station to station while taking notes. Students will be given clues at their station that will lead them to a specific station and so on, or students will read instructions on the board and go blindly to a station of their choice. If they are incorrect, they will continue to solve the clues from station to station. In the end, each group will be tested if they were able to solve all the clues successfully.

Run multiple games:

While I (Brian) don't often create multiple versions of games the way that Kristen does, I do often run two or three of the same game simultaneously. This will allow my groups to be smaller to increase engagement. Having played games with both students and adults that have ranged in size from five to fifty, large groups tend to leave people on the fringes. That does not mean students become a behavior issue, but it does mean they are less engaged in exploring the content you've included in the game. One potential fix for working with large groups is to split them into teams and give them separate sections of the challenge to work out together. Then, the teams can come together when they have solved their portions to help open the box. If, instead, you can run multiple games, it is helpful to create spaces in the room where only that team will find their materials. Ensure there are clear boundaries for people to know where one game ends and the other area begins. Also, create a place for teams to put the locks and clues when they are finished. This will enable you to see what replacement materials you will need, get locks ready to reset as quickly as possible, and make resetting the game easier if you have future classes playing the same game.

If you have multiple classes using the boxes, it might be best to purchase additional boxes or use half for one class and a half for another. This will give you the chance to reset the first set of boxes before the next class. We don't want this to become tiresome for teachers but a learning experience for all.

Challenges:

One of the biggest challenges with creating physical games is set up and then, if necessary, resetting the game. Resetting the game after each class can become tiresome and unnecessary if you have a larger number of boxes. If there are clues that are completed after they are solved, have students place them to the side (or in envelopes, if there are any) so that it will be easier to reset instead of attempting to reassemble the clues, the locks, and the boxes. Additionally, remind students not to play with the locks after they are opened. Changing the combination as they solve other clues will take more time to lock the boxes again.

1. If you plan to play the game in multiple class periods, we would recommend running through the setup one or two times just so you are familiar with where you want everything to go quickly. We have found that multiple boxes with multiple clues and combinations can get mixed up easily. Focus on each box with all its components and attempt to solve them as students would.
2. Keep the game web, planning page, or summary of the game handy to glance at when you are resetting materials. If you are setting something up for the first time, make sure you walk through how your players will get from one to the next to ensure the process connects and you don't have students missing a vital piece of information. By doing this, you will be able to find any issues or problems with any of the clues, combinations, or locks.
3. Practice, practice, practice. Make sure that you practice resetting the locks at least twice. Most of the locks that come with the official kit are extremely easy to reset, but some of the locks you might buy yourself can be tricky, especially the directional lock. If you set (or reset) the directional lock incorrectly, you will not be able to open it again. This type of lock cannot be easily broken into or reset without the correct combination. Being prepared to reset locks in case there are any accidents is a great way to be ready. You must instruct your students not to reset the locks either or play

with them. They can accidentally reset one of the combinations without realizing it. We found that having extra locks on hand will be beneficial and less time consuming in case the students run into any problems.

4. Within game management, it's always essential to have backups of any potentially consumable materials available for use. Whether you are playing a single session game or one that needs to be reset many times, it is vital to make sure that you are prepared with backups for anything that you may need. I have had situations where locks have jammed on a three-digit lockbox, or where I thought would be a perfect place to conceal a clue ended up destroying it as kids were trying to get it free from its hiding place. Backups are a great way to ensure that a game runs smoothly. Also, pay close attention to any problems students may have so that they can be fixed or altered for the next class. When there is time, you can reconfigure the issues students had that day.

Another major challenge when creating your physical games is converting the meaningful content into code that can be input into a lock and used to open the physical box. Unlike using a more open form of digital media to create the lock, using actual locks creates another layer to the challenge both for those trying to solve the puzzles and those trying to create them. This can be done with all kinds of tools. Give students various ciphers, plotting points on graphs, word searches, blackout poems, dates, patterns, maps, and more.

For one of the breakout boxes, a smaller toolbox was bought and locked with a 3-digit lock then it was placed inside the larger toolbox. Under the smaller box was a picture of a famous painting that was mentioned in the book. The students had to find the page number that the painting was mentioned to open the smaller toolbox.

Another way to be creative with lock combinations is to use colored pens or quotes from novels. To make it more challenging, you can have two quotes on one sheet of paper with a "+" sign, where the students have to add the two-page numbers together to solve the lock combination. The opportunities to create combinations and clues are endless.

A creative way to use the directional lock is to use the UV writing pen and write directions on a whiteboard. This was done to a timeline that was on the board. The clue was on the envelope where students had to use the UV light on the whiteboard to find the correct set of directions. However, to make it a little more challenging, there were multiple directions on the board along with directions that would not be used; these are called a 'red herring.' This way, students could not just shine the light just anywhere on the board. The importance of the breakout lesson is not just to solve all the clues, but to understand and learn from them. Remember, think about what the purpose was to create the activity in the first place. See the appendix for ways to create lock combinations, clues, or other ways to be creative. Figure 6.8 explains how to use the Pigpen Cipher code in a breakout game.

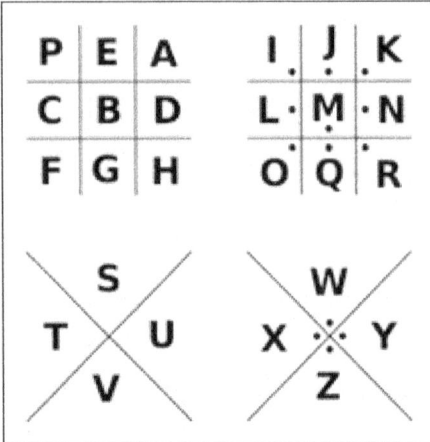

Figure 6.8 The Pigpen Cipher code is a favorite to use at any level to solve a clue. For the younger students, the symbols can spell out a word leading to a word lock or lead to a second clue that will have a combination for a lock. For junior high and high schoolers, you can also use this for a directional lock by only using the letters as directions to figure out the lock. During a unit, symbols from the pigpen cipher were laminated on the wall. The students did not know why they were there until the activity where the cipher code was printed out.

While the Pigpen Cipher code can be a bit more challenging than others, you need to create an activity that fits your class. You can challenge them or stay true to their knowledge. To ensure students stay focused, do not have more than one or two challenging solutions or the students will want to give up. Giving students easy to solve clues is not "dumbing down" the activity, or creating clues that are almost impossible to solve won't help either.

The Hybrid. What is it? Why go Hybrid?
Ideas/Strategies/Challenges

Once you understand the concepts and pieces that go into both physical and digital breakout games, you can start to weave the two together in creating hybrid games. In many cases creating and playing physical games is impractical for the number of students you have in a group. While many games say that you can play with groups of as many as 30, playing a physical game with more than ten students creates significant challenges. In addition to the number of players in a given game, there can also be limitations on the space in your classroom, the availability of physical materials, and the amount of time it takes to plan for and set multiple boxes up in a given game. Conversely, creating digital games provides the opportunity for smaller groups, working games in tighter spaces, and requiring no physical materials other than the technology needed to run the game. If you have played well-developed digital games, there is usually something missing in both the excitement and the ability to move around and be more physically active during the game. One of the things we have noticed in our classrooms has been just how much kids love cracking an actual lock and opening up a box. So to meet a need in the classroom, the hybrid game was born.

Hybrid games are precisely what you think they would be. They are games with significant online or digital components, but that either culminate with or include at least one physical lock and box. The physical component can be the ending, which is a great way to start using a hybrid breakout game. In that case, the box represents a physical ending. It can also be part of a longer process, meaning the box redirects users toward something online. There are several advantages, as we have mentioned in creating hybrid games. The first is that a hybrid game can be played in a class of 30 with groups of 3-5 students. By creating smaller groups, you provide a greater opportunity for interaction and problem-solving. Larger groups also create the possibility for group members to remain on the periphery and take a less active role in being effective problem solvers. By developing a game that includes both digital and physical content, we can get more games played in a smaller space with fewer materials and game resets necessary. Many times, with larger groups, multiple clues were given as a game begins. This allows students to share in the tasks in solving the clues.

One of the biggest challenges to running hybrid games with a small number of materials will be the inevitable log jam of players wanting to use the physical materials. This is solved using the same simple ticket system we use at the deli counter. There are many potential ideas for creating hybrids, some of which we will share in this book.

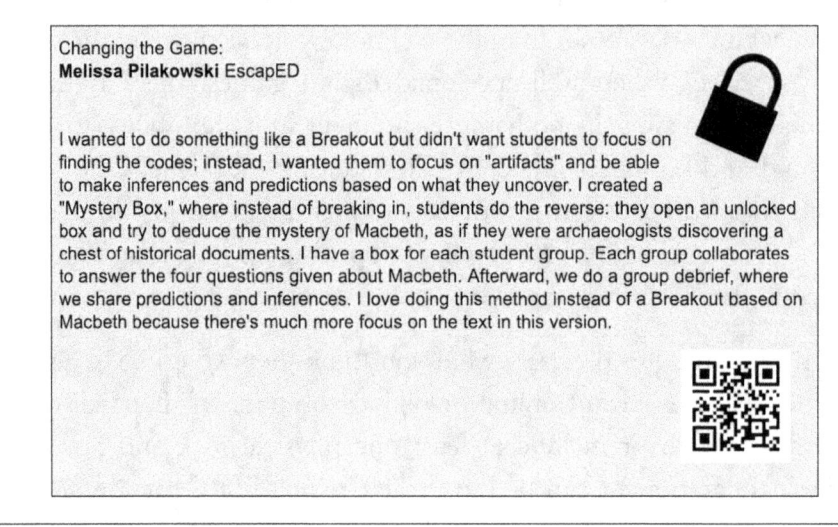

Changing the Game:
Melissa Pilakowski EscapED

I wanted to do something like a Breakout but didn't want students to focus on finding the codes; instead, I wanted them to focus on "artifacts" and be able to make inferences and predictions based on what they uncover. I created a "Mystery Box," where instead of breaking in, students do the reverse: they open an unlocked box and try to deduce the mystery of Macbeth, as if they were archaeologists discovering a chest of historical documents. I have a box for each student group. Each group collaborates to answer the four questions given about Macbeth. Afterward, we do a group debrief, where we share predictions and inferences. I love doing this method instead of a Breakout based on Macbeth because there's much more focus on the text in this version.

When finding places to "hide" clues or combinations to locks, be creative in using objects around the classroom. Even though students might see the most common objects in the classroom, they would not expect them to be part of the breakout game. Here are some images of objects that were used in a regular classroom during a breakout activity.

ESCAPE ED 53

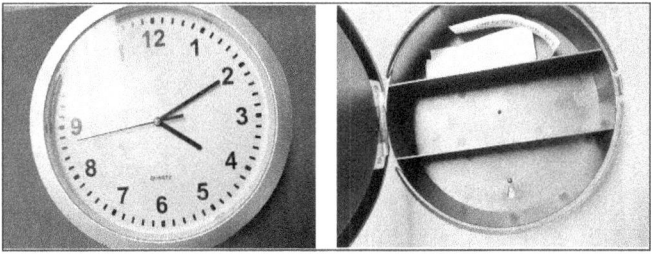

Figure 6.9 - This is a working wall clock with a secret compartment that can be used to hide clues in both physical and hybrid games.

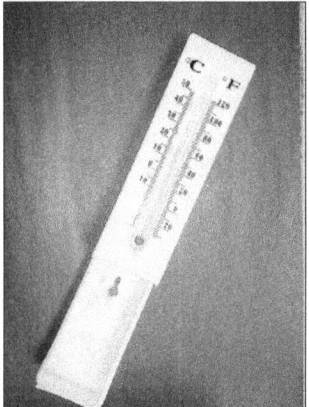

Figure 6.10 - A working room thermometer with a hidden key hook used in physical and hybrid games.

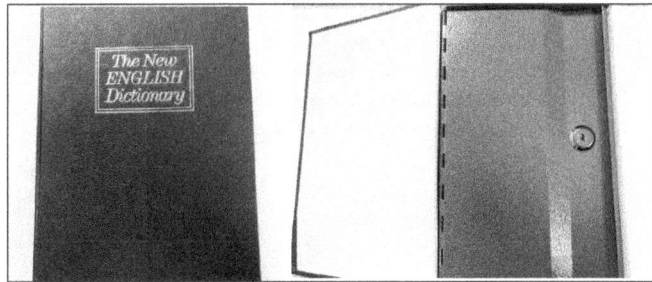

Figure 6.11 - A fake dictionary with a lockable compartment that can be used in physical and hybrid games.

Figure 6.12 - This is a puzzle box. It has no clear opening but two separate compartments that can be used to hide clues and keys.

Figure 6.13 - This is a photo frame bought at a craft show with a clip at the top. I (Kristen) bought six of these to use for my game. A photo was attached to the front of the frame relating to the novel; on the back, there was a code that students had to decipher to find the combination or key to the lock. I gave students the key to decipher the code earlier in the game.

Creating Ideas for a Breakout Lesson

Creating Ideas for a Breakout Lesson

Battle of the Books.
Grayson McKinney Ed. S EscapED

Of all the reasons that motivated me to become a teacher, taking part in a competitive reading program called Battle of the Books was one of the biggest. As an upper primary student attending Lakeside Elementary in East Grand Rapids, Michigan, I was automatically enrolled in this event and put onto a team of about six other students during one afternoon in our library class. We were presented with a list of books that we were to divvy up and devour before the date of the competition. If you've ever participated in pub night trivia, you know the feeling of excitement and camaraderie you get when working together as a team to prove you know your stuff. Subtract the pints of beer and add some cartons of chocolate milk; replace general knowledge with questions about the book list, and you've got yourself... Battle of the Books.

Even today, I live for all of these little "extras" that come with the job. Sure, I love making writing and math feel important and engaging for my students, but I look forward to the special events like field trips, safety squad bowling parties, and reading competitions as much as (or more than) the kids do! I knew that as soon as I became a teacher with a class of my own, I would institute a Battle of the Books competition for my kiddos. Little did I know that our "text-based trial", in particular, would soon become "B" to the 3rd power: *Battle*, *Books*, and *Breakout*!

Now, it's a rare thing to walk away from a PD session feeling motivated to go forth and put into action the ideas that were just presented. In fact, it was shared in a study that while ninety percent of teachers surveyed reported having participated in sessions of professional development during their school year, most of them also reported that it was totally useless (Darling-Hammond et al, 2009). But after attending a professional development session at Michigan State University's 2016 College of Education Technology Conference, I left one particular session feeling so inspired, excited, and totally pumped up to put what I had just learned into practice as soon as possible. What got me so excited? You guessed it: BreakoutEDU!

This educational movement introduced me to something so unique and innovative that I knew right away I had to bring it back to my students. I saw using the immersive Breakout platform as something that could be used for a wide variety of purposes and audiences, and more importantly as the perfect final round to our school's newly introduced Battle of the Books craze. While teaching teamwork, I would also be using the Breakout box to test students' complex problem-solving in the context of the stories they had read.

The first two rounds went as you would expect. Teams gathered around their stations. Posters taped to the front of each table touted their team emblems such as The GoodReads Griffins, The Book Banshees, and Four Princess Unicorns (and Josh). They answered multiple-choice questions on their reading in round one and expounded with open-ended answers in round two. They earned points for correct answers. We kept score. Cookies and hot cocoa were served. It was awesome! But at last came round three: the breakout.

I created clues and hints that stemmed from each of the ten titles they had read, using combinations of puzzles that involved page numbers, quotes from the books, and putting events of books in sequential order. Among the books from that first year, one title especially inspired code-breaking and critical thinking: *Escape from Mr. Lemoncello's Library*. Needless to say, it was an immersive experience in which students could feel like they were actually *in* the coolest library in the world, working together with their teammates (and against their competitors) to crack the codes and win the day! The principles of BreakoutEDU really made this reading experience a memorable one, and in my humble opinion, it was worth every broken lock and lost key incurred along the way. If you're looking for an engaging way to get kids excited about reading,

Darling-Hammond, Linda & Wei, Ruth & Andree, Alethea & Richardson, Nikole & Orphanos, Stelios. (2009). Professional Learning in the Learning Profession: A Status Report on Teacher Development in the United States and Abroad. Accessed on January 16, 2020, from https://www.researchgate.net/publication/237327162_Professional_Learning_in_the_Learning_Profession_A_Status_Report_on_Teacher_Development_in_the_United_States_and_Abroad

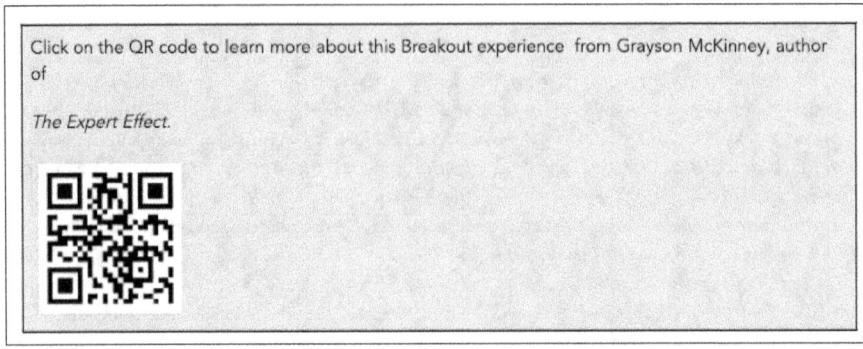

Click on the QR code to learn more about this Breakout experience from Grayson McKinney, author of

The Expert Effect.

While the clues, the story, and the materials will always be important, without those basic lesson essentials, you will not have a quality game nor a valuable learning experience for your participants. Before you get into the fun, before heading down the rabbit hole of game making, it is important to understand the essentials.

Ideas for an introduction:

1. Create an introduction video. The teacher has instructions on the board for students to wait for the video. I (Kristen) had a video of my 9-year old son dressed in a creepy costume covering his body and face. He read a brief script where I used a voice changer as an added effect. He read the directions to start the game. Once he stopped, the timer automatically started on the projection screen. For a different game, another video that was created was having the neighborhood kids each say something different about the novel leading to key events to begin the game. These instructions were given through the video that was played on the projector screen in front of the classroom. There was no instruction from the teacher to start the game. Once the video ended, the clock began to count down.
2. Create instructions with supplementary material in a large manila envelope and leave one at each box. The classroom

bell rings with the timer starting to countdown, and students will need to work together by forming groups or have names or group numbers by each of the locked boxes before class. Students will take out all the material as they figure out which clues to solve first to find the combinations for the locks. To give them a hint, numbers can be written on the back of all the clues to provide the order in which they need to complete the clues. However, I would not give that hint away unless time was running out.

3. Create a QR code to start the game (if smartphones or other technology can be used during class). The QR code will give the students instructions or their first clue on where the instructions are located within the classroom to begin. Be as creative as you need to be in order for students to be engaged. All you will need is a QR code by the box with no other instructions. While this may seem simple, critical thinking is essential when no further instructions are given.
4. For those with a flair for the dramatic, introduce the scenario in character. With each game, there is a storyline involved, so take that storyline and start your class as they enter the room.
5. Have the instructions visible in front of the box, on the board, or verbally give them to the students before the timer begins.

How to create clues:

- Use fake text messages for students to unscramble or read. The messages are clues to a combination of one of the locks or can be a clue that leads to another clue. (https://ifaketextmessage.com)
- Create fake concert tickets. These can be created online and printed out. I would laminate the tickets to avoid them

getting ripped so they can be used for future use. (http://www.faketicketgenerator.com)

- Create fake headlines and newspaper articles. This is an excellent way for students to be actively engaged in reading while learning how to find clues. Clues can be hidden anywhere within the article or headline or certain words can be marked with invisible ink, and students need to use the blacklight flashlight to solve the code. (https://www.fodey.com/generators/newspaper/snippet.asp)
- Using secret messages for students to decipher. These clues can lead to additional clues or the combination to a lock. Kristen created a website focusing on different active learning activities she created to increase motivation. Types of secret messages: (https://kristenkoppers.wixsite.com/diteaching/breakout-boxes)
- Creating an algorithm is an excellent way for students to collaborate to solve. It does not have to be complex to understand. The difficulty of algorithms can vary depending on how much time you want the students to take. A simple one could be just reading a list of directions in order to complete a task to understand or be a more complex riddle to solve by using a cipher code or set of codes. However, communication is the key to solving an algorithm where students learn problem-solving skills.
- Use assignments as clues. For the novel *Chronicle of a Death Foretold* by Gabriel Garcia Marquez, students could use their novels as supplementary material to solve a clue. Students were given information from the novel (numbers) to solve one of the 4-digit lock combinations. By using this method, students are reviewing the material read in class while collaborating with classmates. Past handouts or assignments are other great methods to use as a review of previous activities.

- Augmented Reality to use as clues. There are many platforms to use augmented reality to solve clues. Students will need a phone, iPad, or something similar to view the object. There are free apps that can be downloaded that will be needed if you use augmented reality. Make sure that you test out the image before using it during class.
- Create a Sudoku puzzle using two different colors of paper. Students will need to collaborate on solving the puzzle to find the correct combination for the lock. To make the puzzle easier, you can offer clues or hints on the back of the papers to make sure the numbers are in the correct order. The answers could be one color of paper, and the numbers adding up could be another color.
- A creative way to add additional clues is by going to *Fake WhatsApp* for chat messages, emails, etc. (http://www.fakewhats.com). On this site, you can create messages and emails about your lesson.
- Collect receipts from purchases or create fake receipts with numbers to use as "decoration" or to use them as a clue to solve for a combination of one of the locks. These can be used as a decoy or code to unlock the boxes.

How to end the game:

Make sure that there is a timer set, and students are aware of how much time they have. It's best to have a timer shown on a projection screen. Students who "break into" the box will want to make sure of its worth. Some teachers place candy when students complete all the tasks. In addition to candy, there are many other interesting things you could include in the box. Use school-based rewards, stickers, or even a chance to access a resource that students will find helpful on a formative or summative assessment while still enjoying the game. This goal will also likely be explored in discussion afterwards. No matter what age group is playing the game, students who solve all the clues and "break-in" the box before the timer runs out become excited. But one thing to remember is that it's about the collaboration and learning that is taking place.

While it can be all too easy to allow students to continue playing the game right up until the end of the time you have (as you will likely be rooting for your students' successes), like with any lesson, having a strong conclusion can tie together the key things you want your kids to take away from the activity. The Breakout EDU kit comes with a whole deck of reflection questions to use with your class so you can keep the game reflections fresh and meaningful. If you don't have that resource, building a class discussion about the game is helpful. A good place to start is to ask kids what they found challenging. From there, see how they connected the pieces to solve each puzzle. Why were those pieces important? Why might I have chosen to incorporate those resources/questions/clues into the solution for a lock? Getting the conversation started will allow kids to talk about what they gained from the game. It is also a good place to discuss with your students the importance of not ruining the game for any future classes (if you are playing with multiple classes). Showing how useful the game is, and also how much care and effort went into creating the game, will let your students know that you expect them to take the secrecy of the activity seriously. Ultimately, when you finish the game with a quality discussion of what happened in the game itself and the thought process of your students, it provides you with great feedback on how to improve your game design.

SETTING UP 'THE GAME'

We have all heard the adage that good lesson planning will take care of classroom behavioral management issues. While there's truth in that, we all know it isn't perfect. One of the incredible benefits of using escape room and Breakout style games is that if created and managed correctly, your students can experience a powerful learning opportunity that engages most or all people involved. There are a few important steps to take that work with setting up your games, the types of games you plan, and how you manage them.

To ensure successful experiences and create the best learning for your participants, the first thing you need to know is what kind of game would work best in your classroom and for your purpose.

Many of the games from Breakout EDU come with both a suggested age range and a suggested number of players. Knowing what is age-appropriate tends to come down to a combination of the content and the literacy skills required. Giving students passages that none of them can read just breeds frustration. While your students will undoubtedly stretch their current skill sets to be successful in the game setting, knowing their breaking point with literacy will be a significant determining factor. Even most math games I (Brian) have created require a certain level of literacy.

Second, and almost equally important, is to understand the type of games that will work best. If you have a one-to-one classroom environment and few or no boxes, using digital formats is best. We both believe that having as many students accessing materials during games is crucial to making successful experiences that lack behavior management issues. Playing a digital game where less than half the students have their device is a recipe for problems. Likewise, having students play the game themselves just because they all have access to their device defeats one of the critical purposes of playing these games, fostering collaboration. When you isolate any of your students in the room during a game, you will find some students getting frustrated and giving up. Even though it is easy to help a group get back on track with a well-timed nudge in the right direction, it is tough to do the same for a large group of individuals.

Meanwhile, many physical games will claim that up to thirty people can play them. Good luck with that. While I don't doubt that you can get thirty people in the same space without doing anything too far off-topic, I have seen this repeatedly fail with adults in groups from fifteen to fifty. When you create experiences for twenty to thirty young people, the goal is engagement with the materials. When you put one set of clues and boxes together for an entire class, you will find several students at a minimum on the outside fringes, not solving, not involved, and not learning as you had hoped. Over the past four years of playing and creating breakouts, I have found that ideally, the best size for physical games is between six and ten, while the best size for a digital game is in groups of three to five. The hybrid game can be most effective when you have fewer boxes than you need for a physical game with close to enough devices for a digital one. You can create a hybrid game that allows you to use both the devices in your room and some of the physical materials that come with your boxes. Regardless of which games you choose, ensuring that you have a good student ratio in your groups is incredibly helpful in ensuring everyone stays engaged in the game.

Once you've decided on an appropriate format for your class and your goals, the next step is to manage the game experience while it is happening. Getting a feel for your students will allow you to run games more effectively and also help you assess their learning at the same time. While we were always told that a really good escape room/Breakout game would have an approximate 50% success rate, we want to create a better rate for our classes. While an even split may suggest a quality level of difficulty for the game, it does not necessarily represent the frustration levels of your students.

You may be thinking, "Isn't that what hint cards are for?" and you'd be right. But, if we are playing this game as a learning experience wrapped around content with which we want our students to explore and engage, then we must focus more on helping them dive into the content through the puzzles. Creating well-placed, subtle suggestions, rather than straightforward hints, can refocus an entire group on a puzzle they might otherwise neglect. Rather than sitting back the whole time in silence, smiling at the masterpiece you've laid before your students, mingle among them, listen to their thought processes, and give subtle guidance when you hear their frustrations coming to a peak. Save the hint card for the most significant pieces your students will need in each puzzle, so when they give it, you generally know how to guide them in the direction they need. While some people might think this defeats the purpose by giving students too much help, the objective is to get students to discuss, collaborate, and engage with content. Once they have reached a high level of frustration, all of those things cease to happen. By offering carefully timed and veiled hints, you promote the continuation of the engagement for your students.

TEMPLATES FOR BREAKOUT LESSONS

The templates on the next few pages are used for teacher's purposes only. These are planning sheets that will help create a successful lesson. Before having the students work on a breakout lesson in class, all the clues and answers need to be written/typed on a form to organize themselves. Once all the clues and answers are recorded, separate pieces of paper will then be with each box.

Title:

Subject:

Objective:

Materials Needed:

CCSS:

End Goal:

This template is used to create the lesson focusing on the objectives, materials needed, standards within your state and/or district, and the end goal(s).

Keeping boxes and clues organized can be a challenge. These templates are to help keep track of the clues and answers before using your game in the classroom. I (Kristen) found that these are helpful when you have more than one clue and/or answer to a box. This will not only help with setting up the game, but it also helps for resetting the game for future use.

FOUR DIGIT LOCK		
BOX	CLUE	ANSWER
Box 1		
Box 2		
Box 3		
Box 4		
Box 5		

THREE DIGIT LOCK		
BOX	CLUE	ANSWER
Box 1		
Box 2		
Box 3		
Box 4		
Box 5		

DIRECTIONAL LOCK

BOX	CLUE	ANSWER
Box 1		
Box 2		
Box 3		
Box 4		
Box 5		

KEY LOCK

BOX	CLUE	ANSWER
Box 1		
Box 2		
Box 3		
Box 4		
Box 5		

WORD LOCK

BOX	CLUE	ANSWER
Box 1		
Box 2		
Box 3		
Box 4		
Box 5		

Character's Name: _____

Complete the puzzle to solve your character's name. Everything you need to complete the puzzle will be in the folder.

Clue 1: To find the clue, you'll need to solve the riddle for the lock.

Clue 2: Some words are easier seen than others. With the help of illumination, you will be on your way.

Clue 3: The clue is not hard to solve if you figured out your character.

Clue 4: Unscrambling the letters will point you in the right direction.

Clue 5: Sometimes it's not about the path but it's about the journey. Focus on the direction that you want to take.

Clue 6: Some clues are not as easy as others. Use the first three clues in the hundreds and thousands spot to figure out the clue.

Clue 7: In order to unlock the 3-digit lock box, you will need to look back at the locks to see the order they were unlocked.

Lock	Code	Description of Clue
3-digit		
4-digit		
Word		
Directional		
Key		
3-digit mini box		
Extra Lock		
Extra Lock		
Extra Lock		
Extra Lock		
Notes:		

This template is used to plan out and store information for physical or digital breakouts (with slight modification). I usually add this table into a slides presentation where each lock name is linked to a resource or in-depth description needed for that lock. By changing the lock type, you can easily use this as a simple way to plan each clue with the lock and code. I also frequently use the web format (shown in Chapter 3) for more complicated physical games.

FAQs of working with Breakout Activities:

With all the games out there, why bother creating my own?

While there are probably thousands of games that currently exist for either digital or physical breakout games, very few are going to be tailored to your specific needs for a lesson. If you are genuinely hoping to integrate this resource as a means to engage students with content, then you will undoubtedly need to be capable of creating your own.

How do I begin creating my own breakout box activity or lesson?

Review the steps mentioned earlier in the book to get a better idea of the goal for the breakout lesson. Searching the web for different ideas or going to Breakout EDU will help if you need some extra ideas. Go to www.BreakoutEDU to purchase games, lessons, templates, and activities.

How do I create templates?

You can create your own template to make sure that your lock and combinations are organized, or you can find templates online to fill in. We've included a few template ideas to help you find your own creative niche.

How do I keep all the lock combinations straight?

Creating a Google Doc with all the lock combinations will organize all the answers.

How often do I use a breakout box activity in the classroom?

To encourage students to participate in the breakout boxes, it's best to design one for each unit (if the units are short, maybe create two a semester or one a quarter). You don't want to do too many, and you don't want only to do one a year.

What do I need to create a beginner breakout activity?

A beginner's breakout box will include the larger box, 3 - 4 locks, clue cards and materials, a hasp, a UV light, and a UV pen. The more you add to your design, clue, and lock combinations, the more complicated it will become. If you are a first-timer, create a simple breakout activity with a 30-minute time limit with a discussion afterward. The more comfortable you get with creating breakout activities, the more complex the activity can be.

How can a breakout box be used as an assessment?

The actual activity does not have to be an assessment. It can be a formative activity leading to the assessment inside the box. Some of the best assessment is done while observing your students solving problems. If you do have a formal assessment inside the box, make sure that all students will be able to solve all the clues to open all the locks.

. . .

Can I use a Breakout box activity before we have covered the material?

Yes. You can absolutely create a unit preview with a breakout activity. The activity will be slightly different in that it won't go into the depth of content, but instead, it will focus on hooking student interest in the upcoming unit.

How often should I create new activities?

New activities can be created as many times as you want. It's important to remember to change the lock combinations and number them so that you can enter a new combination. If you lose a lock combination, you will need to purchase new locks.

How do I prepare for my first breakout game?

Your first time running a game can be a little intimidating. The first thing I would do is double-check all your locks. Make sure they are set correctly. Then I would run down a checklist of things that you need to do to set up the game. Double-check to ensure you have all of the clues and important game features set up where they need to be. Finally, once it is all set up, try to step back and have fun.

REFERENCES

Harrington-Atkinson, T. (2017). MBTI introverts learning styles. Paving the Way. Retrieved on February 4, 2021, https://tracyharringtonatkinson.com/mbti-introverts-learning-styles/.

Maslow, A.H. (2013). A theory of human motivation. Mansfield Centre: Martino Publishing.

Rauch, J. (2003). Caring for your introvert. *The Atlantic Monthly*. Retrieved on February 4, 2021.

Romano-Arrabito, C. (2017). To build teamwork, Breakout EDU challenges students to think out of the box. Edsurge. Retrieved on July 21, 2019.

Sanders, Bellow, Harju, Hammonds, & Brucker. (2019). Breakout EDU. Retrieved December 1, 2019, from Breakout EDU website: https://www.breakoutedu.com/learnmore

About the Authors

Kristen Koppers NBCT, M.Ed.

Kristen Koppers is a blogger, presenter, self-published author, and high school educator, as well as an adjunct professor at the local junior college. She has been teaching for eighteen years and is currently teaching high school English in Illinois. She was certified in 2009 as a National Board Certified Teacher (NBCT) and renewed her certification until 2029, having a Master's certificate in teaching. Kristen has a Master's degree in English and a second in Education Administration. Kristen wrote the book *Differentiated Instruction in the Teaching Profession* as a way to share her ideas of how to use Differentiated Instruction inside the classroom by changing *how* we teach, not what we teach. She also wrote a children's book, *The Perfect Puppy*, (#theperfectpuppyedu). As an educator, she believes it is important to find innovative ways to meet the needs of her students.

Kristen is often on Twitter (@Mrs_Koppers), participating in chats and collaborating with other educators. It's easy to share DI ideas on Twitter (#DITeaching). Website: (https://kristenkoppers.wixsite.com/koppers)

Brian Costello

Brian is an educator, author, speaker, and business owner in Southern New Jersey. He currently works with middle school students in robotics and computer science, and has worked in education for 15 years. Brian holds Master's degrees in Elementary Education and School Administration. Brian is the author of *The Teacher's Journey*, a book about learning to control our journey through education through connections, mentoring, reflection, and understanding ourselves. Brian is also the host of a podcast by the same name. Through the podcast, Brian helps share the journeys of other educators by giving them a platform to discuss their successes and struggles. He is also the author of the *Will McGill* series, which are chapter books focused on the challenges of growing up. As an educator, Brian focuses on supporting other educators, advocating for mentoring, exploring emerging technology, and giving kids a broader world experience. You can contact Brian on Twitter (@btcostello05) or see his website www.costellocorner.com.

ALSO BY KRISTEN KOPPERS

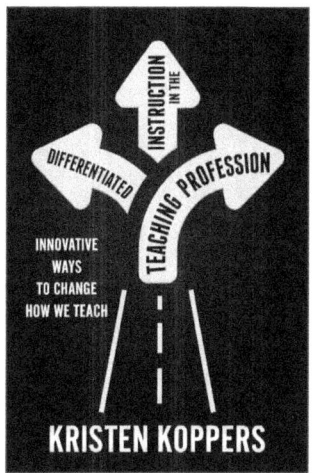

Differentiated Instruction in the Teaching Profession is an innovative way to use critical thinking skills to create strategies to help all students succeed. This book is for educators of all levels who want to take the next step into differentiating their instruction.

Many times we often judge others before we learn about them. In *The Perfect Puppy*, Abbey Mae learns how it feels to not be accepted by others. Follow her journey as she finds out who she is on the inside.

ALSO BY BRIAN COSTELLO

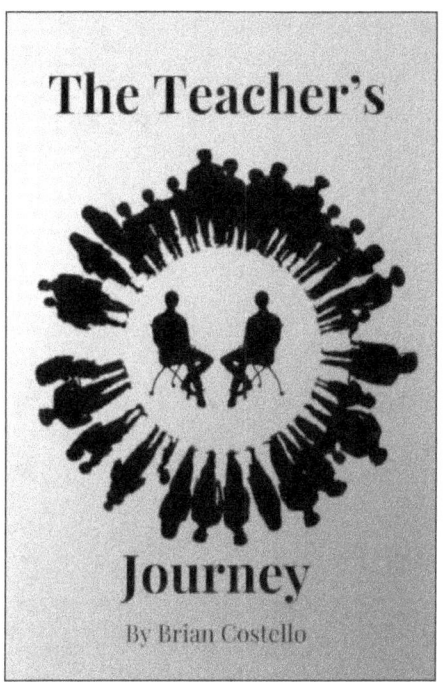

Follow *The Teacher's Journey* with Brian as he weaves together the stories of seven incredible educators. Each step encourages educators at any level to reflect, grow, and connect. *The Teacher's Journey* will ignite your mind and heart through its practical ideas and vulnerable storytelling.

www.ingramcontent.com/pod-product-compliance
Lightning Source LLC
Chambersburg PA
CBHW071422070526
44578CB00003B/654